Think for Yourself

A Kid's Guide to Solving Life's Dilemmas and Other Sticky Problems

b

Think for Yourself: A Kid's Guide to Solving Life's Dilemmas and Other Sticky Problems

Published by Lobster Press™
1620 Sherbrooke Street West, Suites C & D
Montréal, Québec H3H 1C9
Tel. (514) 904-1100 • Fax (514) 904-1101 • www.lobsterpress.com

Publisher: Alison Fripp
Editors: William Mersereau & Alison Fripp
Cover Design & Production: Tammy Desnoyers
Inside Text Layout: GD Grafex Dezine

Distributed in the United States by:
Publishers Group West
1700 Fourth Street
Berkeley, CA 94710

Distributed in Canada by:
Raincoast Books
9050 Shaughnessey Street
Vancouver, BC V6P 6E5

We acknowledge the financial support of the Government of Canada through the Book Publishing Industry Development Program (BPIDP) for our publishing activities.

We acknowledge the support of the Canada Council for the Arts for our publishing program.

National Library of Canada Cataloguing in Publication

MacGregor, Cynthia, 1943 -
Think for yourself : a kid's guide to solving life's dilemmas and other sticky problems / Cynthia MacGregor ; illustrated by Susan Norberg Farias

ISBN 1-894222-73-3

1. Ethics--Juvenile literature. 2. Children--Conduct of life--Juvenile literature. I. Farias, Susan Norberg II. Title.

BJ1631.M33 2003 j170'.83 C2003-902655-8

Printed and bound in Canada.

For Justin, Tori, Steffan, and Aiden – with love

TABLE OF CONTENTS

Introduction 6

Part 1:
Dilemmas with Your Friends 11

Part 2:
Family Dilemmas 47

Part 3:
Dilemmas with Grownups 67

Part 4:
Everyday Dilemmas 77

Conclusion:
Getting a Handle on Other Dilemmas 87

Help! (and where to find it)
Handy Hotlines and Web Sites 93

INTRODUCTION

Uh-oh.

How many times have you said that to yourself: "Uh-oh"? And don't you hate the feeling that goes with it? That "uh-oh" feeling comes when you're facing a *dilemma* – a word meaning a problem that you don't have an answer for right away. A "What-am-I-supposed-to-do-now?" problem.

Life is full of problems, isn't it? Small ones. Big ones. Sometimes you know what the answer is to a problem. Maybe you don't *like* the answer, but you know what you're supposed to do. Like when your friend asks you to help him cheat on a test. You know you're supposed to say "No." The problem here is finding a way to say "No" without seeming like a bad friend. This is what is called a Dilemma.

The idea behind this book is to help you learn how to deal with life's dilemmas. I can't think of every problem you're likely to encounter. Everyone's life is different. But what I can do is to give you some examples of some more common dilemmas for kids your age and then provide you with some suggestions on how to solve them. Hopefully then, the next time you are faced with a dilemma of your own, you can remember some of my problem-solving techniques.

So whenever that "uh-oh" feeling takes over, stop and think of these four things:

1 – Accept the problem you have. Ignoring it isn't going to make it go away. And to put off dealing with it will actually make it worse in some cases.

2 – Think about the possible ways to deal with it and then decide if one of these is the right way.

3 - Then have to courage to act on your decision to solve this dilemma.

4 – And finally, give yourself a huge pat on the back. Dealing with problems or dilemmas is NEVER easy. You should congratulate yourself.

Now, what are the kinds of dilemmas kids mostly face?

• Some are manners problems. I don't mean stuff like remembering to say "Please" or to use a tissue and not your sleeve to wipe your nose. I mean things like having to find a polite way thank someone for something you don't like without hurting their feelings.

• Some are what you might call moral problems. By this I mean situations where you should not do things you think, or know, are wrong. What I said about your friend asking you to help him cheat on a test is an example of this kind of dilemma.

Sometimes you're not sure what the right thing is to do. Other times you're pretty sure of what you need to do – or not do – but it's tough to figure out how to go about doing it (or not doing it).

• Some dilemmas fall into other categories, or they are a combination of manners and morals.

Dealing with the Dilemma

Sometimes the best way to solve a dilemma is to take apart the problem in your mind. Ask yourself:

• Just what is the dilemma?

• Why is it a dilemma?

• Maybe you think of a solution. Great. But what if you realize it isn't a good one? If that's the case, what is the problem with that solution?

• Now that you've figured out what's wrong with your solution, is there a way to get around the problem so that it will make the solution a better one? Maybe you were on to something, and you just need to fine-tune your solution a little!

Too bad your school doesn't have a class in dilemma-solving. That would be a lot more useful than some of the stuff you have to study, wouldn't it? Well, this book can help you learn... and there's no pop quiz or grading!

Now let's look at some real-life dilemmas and see what possible solutions you might come up with.

PART 1

Dilemmas with Your Friends

DILEMMA 1

You are invited to a party at your friend's house. You know that both boys and girls will be there. Your mom asks if there is going to be a parent there, and you ask your friend. Your friend says yes. When you get there though, her parents aren't there. They have left your friend's older sister, who is sixteen, supervising the party.

Why is this a dilemma?

You know your mother believes there is a parent watching over the party. She probably wouldn't approve of your being there with only a sixteen-year-old in charge.

If you think of a solution, but it isn't a good one, what is the problem with that solution?

You could stay at the party and be sure not to do anything your parents would disapprove of. When you got home, you could tell your mom that there was no parent present after all, but that you were careful not to do anything wrong.

But you know your mom probably doesn't want you there without proper parental supervision.

Is there a way around the problem?

The most honorable thing to do is to ask to use the phone and then call your parents. Tell them honestly just what the situation is. Promise that if they let you stay, you won't do anything they'd disapprove of. Promise, too, that you'll call them if the party gets wild or out of hand. Then ask if they'll let you stay under those circumstances.

Maybe they'll respect you enough for your honesty in calling them, and they'll let you stay at least part of the evening. If not, and they insist on your coming right home, you'll still have earned their trust by calling them and telling them the situation.

DILEMMA 2

Your friend didn't study for the Math test today. You almost always get A's in Math. Now your friend wants you to pass him the answers so he won't fail.

Why is this a dilemma?

You don't want to be a cheater, but you don't want to be a bad friend. You also don't want your friend to be mad at you, but if you refuse to help him, he won't be very happy with you.

If you think of a solution, but it isn't a good one, what is the problem with that solution?

You could cheat anyhow, to be a good friend, but you might get caught. Even if you didn't get caught, you wouldn't feel very good about yourself.

You could refuse to help him and tell him it's his own fault if he didn't study, but you know he doesn't want to hear a lecture.

Is there a way around the problem?

You could tell him you won't cheat because if you get caught you'll be in trouble. You don't want him to fail the test, but if you get caught cheating, the teacher will fail you too. Point out to him that that wouldn't be fair to you, would it? Now you're not lecturing him, nor are you refusing just because it's wrong to cheat. You're protecting yourself. He should understand that at least a little better.

Maybe you can offer to help him some other way. You could go over some math problems together, quickly, right now, before school starts. Maybe you could offer to help him study for the next test, if he doesn't like studying alone.

By offering something in return, you're not just flatly refusing to help him. You're showing that *you* are being a good friend. And if he's really a friend, and not a mooch, then he's probably a lot less likely to be angry if you take this approach.

DILEMMA 3

You go to a friend's birthday party and find that some of the kids there brought alcohol and are drinking it secretly in the basement.

Why is this a dilemma?

There are two problems with there being alcohol at the party. One: It's illegal. You're all underage. If somehow the police find out and come to break up the party, you could get in trouble too. Two: You are a bit scared. What if these kids get out of control? Or what if they ask you to drink too and you don't want to. Three: Your parents would kill you if they knew you were at a party where there's any kind of drinking.

If you think of a solution, but it isn't a good one, what is the problem with that solution?

You could stay at the party and just refuse to drink anything yourself. But you know that your parents' objection isn't only because you might take a drink. They're really concerned because they know (and so should you) that kids your age can't handle drinking. Even if they have just a couple of beers, things might get out of hand; it really isn't a good, safe place for you to be.

Is there a way around the problem?

You really need to leave the party. And not just to please your parents. Kids and beer don't mix. You need to leave *for your own safety*. Things could get messy, and you don't need to be in the middle of it... or be a victim. Call your parents, tell them what's going on, and ask them to come and get you.

They'll respect you for it!

HAPPY BIRTHDAY
BEER
Soda
Cola

DILEMMA 4

You go over to a friend's house to watch videos. When you get there, your friend's older brother and his friends are watching X-rated videos. They invite you to join them. You know your parents don't want you watching anything X-rated.

Why is this a dilemma?

To begin with, you've never seen an X-rated movie, and you'd like to for once. Besides, if you say you won't watch because your parents wouldn't like it, your friend's brother and his friends might call you a wimp or a wuss.

If you think of a solution, but it isn't a good one, what is the problem with that solution?

You *could* watch the videos and just not tell your parents. Then you wouldn't get in trouble... and, after all, what's the big deal about watching a couple of videos? But if you did that, and your parents ever found out somehow, they wouldn't trust you as much. Besides, you know you're not supposed to. You were raised to know the difference between right and wrong, and you know that watching a movie you're not supposed to watch is simply wrong, no two ways about it.

Is there a way around the problem?

You need to stand up for what you know is right, even if someone calls you a name. Tell the other kids, "Sorry, but I'm not allowed to watch X-rated movies."

But suppose one of the kids wants to be mean and says something like, "Do you always do everything your mommy tells you?"

If he does, you can say, "I'm not sneaking behind my parents' backs. That's why they trust me. I've worked hard to earn their trust, and I'm not gonna mess up now." Take pride in being honorable. No matter what anyone says, you know you're doing the right thing. And, no matter what they say, the other kids know it too!

Dilemma 5

You suddenly realize that you've made plans to meet with two friends for the same day. When Lynn invited you to come over after school Tuesday, and you agreed, you totally forgot that you'd already made a plan with Kayla for that afternoon. What a mess! You weren't trying to hurt anyone's feelings, but now it looks like you're going to have to cancel on someone.

Why is this a dilemma?

You want to see both your friends. And you don't want to hurt Kayla's feelings by saying you're getting together with Lynn, but you don't want to hurt Lynn's feelings by saying you're going over to Kayla's house.

If you think of a solution, but it isn't a good one, what is the problem with that solution?

You could cancel your plans with both of them and reschedule each for a different day, but then you might hurt both their feelings *and* you mess up your own afternoon.

Is there a way around the problem?

If your mom doesn't mind your having two friends over on Tuesday afternoon, you could tell both Kayla and Lynn that you messed up and made two dates for the same day, but that you'd like them both to come to your house instead.

But maybe your mom said No. Or maybe Kayla and Lynn don't get along well together. In that case, you have to figure out which friend you made the date with first. Then you have to tell the other one that you're sorry, but you messed up, and you need to reschedule your date for some other time.

People make honest mistakes. This was one. Nobody should get angry with you over it.

DILEMMA 6

The gym teacher always puts Kyle, the slowest runner, or the worst player, on your softball team. It seems you just can't win with Kyle on your team.

Why is this a dilemma?

You want to win, but you can't with him on your team. You don't like always losing.

If you think of a solution, but it isn't a good one, what is the problem with that solution?

You could complain to the teacher that it's not fair for you to always be stuck with Kyle on your team. But if Kyle hears you complaining, you'll hurt his feelings.

Is there a way around the problem?

There are at least two possibilities.

One is to talk to the teacher some time other than in class. Point out that the teacher *always* puts Kyle on your team and that, because of him, it's very hard for you to win. Without whining, tell the teacher that the game is much more fun when there's a fair chance of winning, and that under these circumstances you have very little chance. The teacher may not even be aware that he always puts Kyle on your team.

The other possibility is to try to help the bad player become better. If Kyle is a slow runner, there's not too much you can do about it, but maybe the problem is that he's not very good at throwing or catching or batting. If that's the case, you can try to help him get better. Give him some pointers on how to play better. Practice with him. Help him. Maybe he just needs some extra encouragement. Maybe he really *wants* to be a better player. He probably doesn't enjoy being the worst player in the class.

If you help him get better, you're solving your own problem and doing a nice thing for someone else.

DILEMMA 7

A kid you really don't like talking to or don't have anything in common with wants to be friends with you. She keeps asking you to come over to her house after school.

Why is this a dilemma?

You don't have the same interests, or you just don't enjoy her company. But she won't take "No" for an answer and keeps asking you. You don't want to just say, "I don't want to spend time with you." You know that would hurt her feelings. But she keeps asking you.

If you think of a solution, but it isn't a good one, what is the problem with that solution?

You could say "Yes" just once, to be polite. But then if she has a good time with you, she's likely to ask to spend time with you more often than ever. And if you don't have a good time, the problem will only have gotten worse.

Is there a way around the problem?

If you just don't like the girl, you'll have to keep saying "No" till she gets the message that you don't want to spend time with her after school. You should really try to be polite to people and not hurt their feelings unnecessarily. This means you should *not* tell her you don't like her. But it doesn't mean you have to spend time with her just to keep from hurting her feelings.

Then again, maybe you're not sure that you dislike her. Maybe you just don't enjoy doing the same things. If that's the case, you could try showing her the things you like. Maybe she could learn to like playing the games you like to play. Maybe she could learn to like doing the things you like to do. It's worth trying once. And if it doesn't work out, you have a very good reason to say "No" the next time she asks you. You could say: "I'm sorry, but I don't like biking and you don't like playing board games. I don't enjoy watching the TV shows you like and you don't like the TV shows I like. You don't like playing volleyball and I don't like playing softball. We just don't like doing the same things."

And here's another thought: Maybe she just doesn't have enough friends. Is there someone else you know who likes the same things she likes? Maybe you could suggest she make an after-school date with this other girl? Maybe your friend Ashley would love to be friends with her? Even if you don't particularly like her, maybe Ashley would. Even if you don't enjoy doing the things she likes, maybe Ashley does. You'll do her a favor by finding her a friend *and* you'll get her off your back.

DILEMMA 8

As you're walking home from the school bus stop, one of your friends pulls out a pack of cigarettes and offers you one.

Why is this a dilemma?

You know your parents will freak if they catch you smoking.

If you think of a solution, but it isn't a good one, what is the problem with that solution?

You could take just a puff or two and make sure not to inhale. That way your friends won't get on your case, which they might if you refuse.

But there are two problems with this. One: You might

find you like smoking, even if you try not to inhale. And then you could get hooked. And you know smoking can kill you. Two: A neighbor might see you and tell your parents.

Is there a way around the problem?

You have to take a stand and firmly decline the offer. Don't put it on the basis of "My parents wouldn't want me to." Instead, stick to health reasons for refusing. You can say, "Cancer? No thanks. I don't want any." Or you can say, "If you want to risk your health, that's your business, but *I* know what cigarettes can do to you." And if you play any sports, you can add, "Besides, cigarettes leave you winded. It wouldn't be good for my soccer game."

DILEMMA 9

Your friend Gene has body odor. At the start of every school day, it's barely noticeable, but it's there. As the day goes on, it gets worse. And by the time gym class is over, he's really rank. Gene's a friend, but not your best bud, and you feel kind of awkward mentioning it to him. On the other hand, it's no fun to smell him, either in school or after school... and he does like to spend time with you after school.

Why is this a dilemma?

You don't like being around Gene because Gene *smells*. You'd like to spend more time with him. You both like shooting hoops. You both like playing video games. But he has a real problem there. You're starting to avoid him because of it.

If you think of a solution, but it isn't a good one, what is the problem with that solution?

You want to help him because he's your friend. If people were keeping away from you for a reason, you'd want someone to let you know. But if you tell him he stinks and he needs to wash better, you'll probably hurt his feelings. Even if you say it in more polite language than that.

You could also leave him an anonymous note in his desk or locker that tells him he has an odor problem. But then he might wonder who left the note and start feeling self-conscious and embarrassed because of it. You don't want to embarrass him by telling him to his face. But when he looks at everyone in class and wonders, "Is this the person who left the note?" he might be more embarrassed than ever.

Is there a way around the problem?

If you know Gene's mom or dad reasonably well, you could try to either go see one of them or call one of them on the phone – when you know Gene's not home. Tell Gene's parent, "Please don't call Gene to the phone – I'm calling to talk to you." Then tell the mom or dad what the problem is. Explain that you don't want to embarrass Gene by saying anything to him. Tell his mom or dad that you're sure some of the kids keep away from him because of the odor problem.

If you can't talk to Gene's parents, maybe your teacher would talk to Gene or his parents. Talk to your teacher and see if he or she will help you.

DILEMMA 10

Your friend likes to shoplift. Your mom has always told you stealing is wrong. Your friend says, "I wouldn't steal from a person. This is different. I'm stealing from a big company. They expect some people to steal. My dad said so. Come with me. We can take some comic books. They'll never catch us. It's fun!" When you say "No," she calls you a loser.

Why is this a dilemma?

Nobody likes their friends to call them names. But you know stealing is wrong. Any kind of stealing... from a person, from a store, any kind of stealing is wrong.

If you think of a solution, but it isn't a good one, what is the problem with that solution?

You could walk out of the store with the comic books, like your friend wants. You could read your comic books carefully, without messing them up, then mail them back to the store without your name on the envelope. You could enclose a note saying you didn't want to take them, and you're returning them. Then the store would have them back and could sell them.

But you're still doing something wrong. You might even get caught. (Don't forget, stores are getting better and better technology to cut down on theft!) And even if you don't get caught, your friend will only want to do the same thing all over again another time. So you really haven't solved anything.

Is there a way around the problem?

You can point out to your friend that stealing is stealing, whether you're stealing from a person or a big company. (Even big companies are still owned by people.) You can also point out that when people steal from stores, it costs the stores money. In order to make back the money they lose from theft, stores have to raise their prices. So by stealing from the store, you're making the prices go up and, in a way, you still have to pay for it.

Maybe your friend will see it your way. Maybe your friend will realize now that stealing is wrong – any kind of stealing. But even if your friend doesn't agree with you, even if she still wants to steal or says you're not being a friend, or you're being a wuss, you need to stand up for what you know is right and do what you know is right.

What's right is to not steal. What's right is to try to make your friend understand that, too. If you walk out of the store without taking anything, and you've tried to keep your friend from stealing, you've done the right thing. This is true regardless of what your friend winds up doing.

DILEMMA 11

Some older kids are always selling drugs (perhaps crack, pot, or Ecstasy) on the corner near the school. So far, you've avoided these kids, but today they approach you.

Why is this a dilemma?

You know that taking drugs can kill you! And you know how easy it is to get hooked if you try it and like it.

And beyond the problem of what the drugs themselves do to you, there's another problem. Drugs are illegal. If you get caught with drugs in your possession, you're in biiiiiiig trouble. Trouble with the law, trouble with your family, and perhaps trouble with your school. You could wind up in jail. You could wind up with a criminal record. You could wind up with your life messed up beyond belief.

Even if you escape getting caught by the police, you still will get "caught" by the drugs – hooked on the addictive drugs or just entirely too eager to smoke pot regularly. And drugs are expensive! Kids who get hooked on drugs often become thieves to get money to buy drugs. So if drugs are being sold in your neighborhood, or near your school, it's way bad. It's bad for the kids, and it's bad for the neighborhood.

If you think of a solution, but it isn't a good one, what is the problem with that solution?

You and your friends could tell the dealer to go sell his drugs somewhere else.

But the dealer might try to do something to you to get even. You could just ignore him and promise each other not to buy any drugs yourselves. But you know some other kids are likely to give in to temptation.

Is there a way around the problem?

This is one of those dilemmas that you need an adult to help solve. You can't fix this problem yourself except by alerting an adult who can do something. Report the dealer to someone appropriate – like the school principal, the police, or even the crossing guard, if there is one nearby.

What if it happens that the dealer is a friend of one of your friends? Then don't tell your friends you're reporting the dealer. Do it quietly. **But do it.** You may be saving one of your friends' life!

Why is this a dilemma?

If you don't go, you may hurt Evan's feelings, and your mom has told you many times that you mustn't hurt people's feelings if it can possibly be avoided.

If you think of a solution, but it isn't a good one, what is the problem with that solution?

You can go anyhow. Two or three hours wouldn't be so awful.

But then maybe Evan will expect you to invite him to

your next party – and probably to make occasional after-school plans with him as well.

Is there a way around the problem?

If this is a party to which all of the class, or a large number of other kids, have been invited, you can go. Since it's not a one-on-one situation, you don't need to spend lots of time alone with Evan. And since many kids will be there, Evan can't expect all of you to become good friends with him. But if you know that not many kids were invited, you might be better off saying "No, thanks."

Anyhow, you would need to check with your mom first. Tell your mom you've been invited to a party you don't want to go to. Ask her to tell you she has other plans for you that day. When she does, you can tell Evan that your mom said "No," you are supposed to be doing something else that day. The "something else" might just be your homework, but *technically* you're not lying.

There are times when half-truths are kinder than the whole truth. Which is better: to say, "I'm staying home and doing my homework" or to say, "I don't want to go to your party"? You may not like Evan, but you don't want to hurt his feelings unnecessarily.

You also don't want to set up the expectation that now you're going to be friends and start hanging together. So wiggling out of it with a half-truth is the kindest thing you can do.

DILEMMA 13

You and your friend find a wallet on the street. You want to try to find the owner and return it to him or else turn it in to the police. Your friend wants to keep the money. He says, "We're not stealing. We didn't take the money. We found it on the street. If we hadn't found it, someone else would have. And they would have kept the money. So we're not doing anything wrong."

Why is this a dilemma?

If you insist on returning the wallet and money, your friend isn't going to be very happy with you. If you give in to him, you aren't going to be very happy with yourself.

If you think of a solution, but it isn't a good one, what is the problem with that solution?

You could let your friend keep the wallet and all the money. That way you yourself aren't guilty of keeping something that isn't yours. But you still would know that someone somewhere is looking for a wallet that belongs to him. And *you* know where that wallet is, but you aren't doing anything about returning it to its owner. And, since you didn't keep any of the money, your friend is still likely to rub it in that you're a nerdy geek.

Is there a way around the problem?

Somebody's going to be unhappy with somebody no matter how you work this out. So isn't it better for you to try to see that the money is returned? That way, even if your friend is unhappy with you, at least you'll feel good about yourself.

And maybe you can even get your friend to see it your way. It's worth a try. Tell him, "Suppose *you* lost your wallet. Wouldn't you like the person who found it to return it to you? Don't you think we ought to do the same thing for the person who lost this wallet?"

You can even add, "Maybe he needs the money desperately. But even if he doesn't, it's his money. We need to return it to him." And you can also say, "Maybe there'll be a reward. That would be money we could keep with a clear conscience. That would really belong to us."

DILEMMA 14

Your best friend, Joey, is running for class president. You really like your best bud, but you think that Kevin Matthews would be a better class president than Joey would.

Joey says, "You're gonna vote for me, aren't you?"

Why is this a dilemma?

Joey thinks you'll vote for him out of friendship. You know Kevin is really the better choice. Do you vote for Kevin and get your best friend mad at you? Do you vote for Joey and know you voted with your heart, not your head?

If you think of a solution, but it isn't a good one, what is the problem with that solution?

You could vote for Kevin and tell Joey that you voted for him. The voting is secret; he'll never know.

Or you could vote for Joey. What's one vote? If Kevin is the better person for class president, he'll probably win anyhow.

First, the problem is you're lying. Second, you are wimping out and not doing what you want to do.

Is there a way around the problem?

If Kevin is the better person for the job, you need to vote for Kevin. If everyone votes for their friends, this will turn into a popularity contest. But it's not a popularity contest; it's an election for an important office.

You don't have to tell Joey – and you don't have to lie, either. You can learn to be diplomatic... the way grownups do it. (You have to learn sometime. You might as well start now.) If Joey asks, "Who did you vote for?" you can answer by laughing and saying, "Who do you think I voted for?" You didn't come right out and say you voted for him. You didn't lie. If he pushes you, say, "I voted for the best person for the job, of course," and smile or even wink at him.

You've saved his feelings, not hurt them. Yet you've voted for the best person. Yes, it's a little less than honest... but it's not *dis*honest. And you've kept from hurting anyone's feelings, which is important, and done what your conscience told you was right.

DILEMMA 15

You've made plans with your friend Jennifer for Friday night. She's going to sleep over, and you plan to rent a movie and stay up late. Her mom doesn't let her do sleepovers very often, so she's been looking forward to this for three weeks.

Then your best friend, Alison, calls you. She's got two free tickets to the ice show and wants you to go with her. The ice show is only going to be in town for three days and the tickets are usually really expensive.

Why is this a dilemma?

You want to go to the show with your best friend, Alison, but you've promised your other friend, Jennifer, you'd spend the time with her.

If you think of a solution, but it isn't a good one, what is the problem with that solution?

You could ask Alison if Jennifer could go with you to the ice show. But Alison's only got two tickets. You could ask Alison to join you and Jennifer for the sleepover; but if she's got the complimentary ice show tickets, she probably can't trade them in for tickets on a different date. You've got a real dilemma here.

Is there a way around the problem?

There's no wonderful solution here. You're going to disappoint one friend... and you're going to be disappointed yourself... no matter which way you choose. You have to either stick with your initial plan and disappoint Alison, or disappoint Jennifer by going to the ice show with Alison.

And, really, a commitment is a commitment. So you'd better stick with your plan with Jennifer. It's unfortunate... but sometimes life is like that. Sometimes there are no wonderful, easy answers that solve everything. And you did have the plan with Jennifer first. And she is counting on spending the time with you.

PART 2

Family Dilemmas

DILEMMA 1

Aunt Eileen has sent you an awful sweater for your birthday. Now your mom wants you to write her a thank-you note, and you don't know what to say.

Why is this a dilemma?

You don't want to lie and say you love the sweater, but you can't tell the truth in the thank-you note and say you hate it.

If you think of a solution, but it isn't a good one, what is the problem with that solution?

You might think of asking your mom to thank Aunt Eileen for you. That way you don't have to say anything to Aunt Eileen. But you know you're supposed to write a note yourself. And your mom wouldn't go along with your not writing one.

If you write Aunt Eileen and tell her you loved the sweater, not only are you lying, but she might send you more sweaters like it in the future! And if you say, "Too bad it's the wrong size and a terrible color," you're being honest, but you'll probably hurt her feelings.

Is there a way around the problem?

Can you find *anything* nice to say about the sweater? Without saying "I really love the sweater you sent me," can you say it's a cheerful color? Can you say it has an interesting pattern? Can you say it's a nice warm sweater? Can you say it was thoughtful of Aunt Eileen to remember your birthday? There! You've said four nice things about the sweater and none of them is dishonest. You haven't actually said you *liked* the sweater. You haven't promised to wear it. And although you haven't told her how you honestly feel about it, you didn't tell any lies.

DILEMMA 2

Your parents don't want you going into chat rooms online. They know the dangers that can come with conversations in some chat rooms. These can range from people simply talking about stuff that's inappropriate for kids your age, all the way to approaches from sexual predators. Unfortunately, adults who have a sexual interest in kids will often spend time in those chat rooms that are of the most interest to kids.

Why is this a dilemma?

All your friends spend time in chat rooms. And you don't like being the only one who doesn't. You want to see what they're talking about. You don't like feeling left out during conversations when they talk about visiting chat rooms and you've never been in one.

If you think of a solution, but it isn't a good one, what is the problem with that solution?

You could point out to your mom that "All the *other*

kids go to chat rooms."

But that "All the other kids do it" argument has never really worked with your parents before.

Is there a way around the problem?

There are some chat rooms that are specifically for kids, and some in which conversations are monitored by a supervisor. Ask all your friends for the URLs (Web site addresses) of any chat rooms like these that they know about. Then give your parents the list. Ask them to check out some or all of these chat rooms and see if they feel comfortable letting you go into them.

DILEMMA 3

All your friends download music from the Internet. Your parents have pointed out to you, though, that when you do that, you're stealing copyrighted material. They have asked you not to download music that way anymore.

Why is this a dilemma?

You want a big music collection like your friends have, but you don't want to have to spend all your allowance on CDs. None of your friends do. They all download music. It seems your choices are either to download it from the Internet against your parents' wishes, to spend all your money on CDs and tapes, or to do without a nice music collection.

If you think of a solution, but it isn't a good one, what is the problem with that solution?

You could copy your friends' tapes and CDs. That way you're not downloading from the Internet sites that your parents asked you to keep away from.

But while you're following the *exact words* of what they said, you know you're not really avoiding what they want you to avoid. You're still pirating.

Is there a way around the problem?

Here's the problem with pirating: Every time you copy a song instead of buying it, you're depriving people of royalties. The music company, the recording artist (singer or group), the person who wrote the song... they all get paid for each copy sold. If nobody paid for their music, nobody would earn any royalties, and soon people would stop writing and recording songs.

The fair thing and the right thing is to buy the tape or CD. Don't buy every album or single you want. Be selective. Get only the ones that you really, *really* like. And you can certainly borrow others from your friends. There's nothing wrong with borrowing.

DILEMMA 4

Somehow the back gate was left open, and your family's dog got loose. The city found him and picked him up, but when your parents got him back, he looked like he'd been in a fight. He had cuts and bite marks all over him.

Not only was the dog hurt, but the whole thing cost your parents money. They had to pay the city to get the dog back, and then there was a bill at the vet's for treating the bites and cuts.

They blamed you. They thought you left the gate open when you brought your bike in and put it in the backyard. You were sure you had latched the gate behind you, but how can you prove it?

Then you went into your sister's room and saw that she'd left her diary out on the bed. Even though you knew you shouldn't, you picked up the diary and read it. In the diary, she wrote that she had left the gate open. While you got blamed for what happened to the dog, it was really your sister's fault.

Why is this a dilemma?

If you tell your parents what you read, you're admitting to reading your sister's diary. Then you'll be in trouble with them and with her. But if you don't tell them, they'll go on blaming you for what happened.

If you think of a solution, but it isn't a good one, what is the problem with that solution?

You could tell your sister that one of your friends saw her leave the gate open, and then she might admit it. But you know you're lying. Besides, if she challenges you, you don't really have a witness.

You could do something nasty or sneaky to her to get even. But your mom always tells you that "Two wrongs don't make a right," and besides, getting even doesn't really solve the problem.

Is there a way around the problem?

You really have only two choices: Admit you read the diary, and get the mess straightened out; or keep your mouth shut, don't get in trouble about reading the diary, and keep on being blamed about the dog.

Wouldn't you rather be in trouble for something you *did* do than for something you're innocent of?

You should own up to reading the diary, and then deal with your sister's anger (and perhaps a few words from your mother about snooping). But at least you'll be cleared of the blame for what happened to the dog.

Maybe next time you won't read her diary. Maybe next time she won't leave the gate open. Maybe next time your parents won't blame you so quickly. Maybe everyone will learn something from this unfortunate incident.

DILEMMA 5

Your mom says you're all going to your grandmother's nursing home for a visit. You love your grandmother, but you hate visiting her because she can never remember who you are. And her home is more like a hospital and smells like one too. You hate hospitals.

Why is this a dilemma?

You love your grandmother and want to see her, and you know you should. But it's no fun to visit someone who doesn't even recognize you. And besides, hospitals freak you out.

If you think of a solution, but it isn't a good one, what is the problem with that solution?

If you have a lot of homework to do, or a big test coming up, your mom might excuse you from going. You could send your grandmother a little present with your family. She doesn't know who you are anymore anyhow!

But you know it can't be fun to live in a place like that, and even if she doesn't remember who you are, surely your grandmother enjoys getting visitors – and the more, the better.

Is there a way around the problem?

If you *really* have a lot of homework or a big test to study for, it would probably be all right to stay home this time. But then you *have* to go next time. If you *don't* really have homework or study commitments, go and see your grandmother. I know it's not fun. It's not fun for your mother either. (It's even worse for her. Grandma is her own mother... and your grandmother probably doesn't recognize your mom either!) But your mom goes to see her anyhow.

Your mom – and you – and the rest of the family can do your best for your grandmother. You can kiss her, talk to her, make sure she's comfortable. You can bring her little gifts she'll enjoy. You can just be there for her.

Someday it might be you in a nursing home. You'll want your family to come visit, won't you? What goes around comes around!

DILEMMA 6

You told your parents you'd returned that library book, but the truth is you lost it. Now the library wants you to pay to replace the book, and you don't have the money for it.

Why is this a dilemma?

You can usually go to your parents when you need money for something legitimate. But, since you told your parents you'd returned the book, you can't ask them for the money.

If you think of a solution, but it isn't a good one, what is the problem with that solution?

You could tell them you need the money for something else, something they'd approve of. But that would only make things worse because now you'd be telling them a second lie on top of the original lie.

Is there a way around the problem?

Go to the librarian. Tell her (or him) that you don't have the money, but you're willing to work your debt out. Tell her you'll do work around the library until you've paid off your debt in labor. Ask the librarian if that will be acceptable.

If it isn't, maybe you can earn money in one of the ways kids have always done it: rake leaves, shovel snow, pull weeds, walk dogs, and do similar chores for neighbors.

Whether the library lets you work off the money or you're earning it through neighborhood chores, tell your parents either way. You need to square things with them. Tell them, "You know that library book I told you I had returned? I guess I was wrong. The library says I never returned it. But I can't find it. So I'm working to pay them back."

And what if all else fails? What if the library won't let you work off what you owe them, and you can't raise enough money by doing chores in the neighborhood? Well, you were going to tell your parents the truth anyhow. So tell them you want to earn extra money from them to pay the library back. Don't just ask them to bail you out. Ask them to advance you the money and to give you extra chores to make it up.

And then be sure to make good on your promise. When your mom or dad asks you to rake leaves, to do laundry, to wash the dog, or to do some other extra chore to earn the money they advanced you, don't groan and complain and don't try to wiggle out of it!

DILEMMA 7

Your friend Ed tells you, "You've got to see what I found on the Web!" It turns out he's talking about a porn site.

Your parents have told you they don't want you going onto that type of Web site. In fact, they have software on your computer that prevents you from accessing that type of site. But Ed's parents don't have any parental controls on their computer.

Why is this a dilemma?

To begin with, Ed's got you curious. In addition, you don't want to look like a wuss by saying, "My parents won't let me."

If you think of a solution, but it isn't a good one, what is the problem with that solution?

If Ed accessed the site, and you were only looking over his shoulder, then technically it wouldn't be *you* who logged on to the site. Or maybe Ed could send copies of a few of the pictures to you at home. That way you'd get a sampling of what's on the site without actually going there.

But you know your parents really don't want you looking at that kind of stuff at all. Even if you're not the one who accessed the site. Even if you're not even viewing the pictures while on the Web but through e-mail.

Is there a way around the problem?

The only right thing to do is refuse to get involved. Not that I don't understand why you want to look. You're curious, and curiosity is natural. But let your curiosity stay unsatisfied a few more years. If you're the age to be reading this book, you're really too young to be visiting porn sites. And that's that.

DILEMMA 8

Your parents are divorced. You see your dad every other weekend, and every other Wednesday. It's really great to see him! You miss him!

He tells you, "You're my helper now. I want to know everything that's going on in the family." And he asks a lot of questions.

Some of the questions are fine. He asks if the lawn is mowed, if you're doing your homework, if everything is OK at home. There's no problem there. But some of his questions make you uncomfortable. He asks about how your mom spends her evenings. He asks you if your mom is dating. He asks if she's going out with anyone.

You don't feel totally comfortable telling him. But he tells you it's nice to know he can count on you to tell him what's going on at home. Dad makes you feel important and grown-up. He tells you you're being a good son or daughter to him.

But you don't feel right about telling him what your mom is doing with her private life. She isn't married to your dad anymore. Is it really his business? Are you being a good son or daughter, like he says? Or are you being a spy and spying on your mom?

Why is this a dilemma?

You want your dad's approval. You like feeling important. But you don't feel right telling him your mom's private business.

If you think of a solution, but it isn't a good one, what is the problem with that solution?

You could tell him what he wants to know. Your mom would probably never know you told him. And it makes you

feel important, and necessary, and helpful, like your dad can really count on you. And isn't that good?

But it also makes you feel like you're letting your mom down. Aren't you being a spy? Aren't you telling your dad what your mom is doing in her private life? And you know that's not really your dad's business anymore. He's not married to your mom anymore. He's still your dad. But he's not your mom's husband anymore.

Is there a way around the problem?

Tell your dad that you won't tell him about your mom's private life... just like you wouldn't tell your mom anything about his private life. Tell him he's making this really hard on you. You're just a kid, but you're old enough to know not to carry stories from one parent to the other. Tell him you're well, and so is your mom, and the house is in good shape, but if he wants to know about your mom's private life, he needs to ask her, not you.

This won't be easy! But if you don't tell him, you're going to have him asking you questions about your mom all the time, and eventually that's going to be harder. You need to be firm. You need to say "No." You need to start now.

PART 3

Dilemmas with Grownups

Why is this a dilemma?

Your mom expects you to be polite to her friends, but this woman's breath is gross, and she has a grip like a boa constrictor. Still, if you try to squirm away from her, your mom won't be very happy.

If you think of a solution, but it isn't a good one, what is the problem with that solution?

You could say, "Thank you, but I don't like to kiss people. " But she might say, "Aw, we're almost family, you can let *me* kiss you!" In that case, you could say, "Don't kiss me. I think I'm catching a cold," but that wouldn't be honest, and you can't use that excuse every time, anyhow.

Is there a way around the problem?

Yes, you can say, "If you don't mind, I'd rather shake hands." This keeps you at a safer distance. And shaking hands is an acceptable alternative.

DILEMMA 2

You'd like to learn to play the guitar, and your parents have agreed to pay for lessons. They suggested you ask the school music teacher for the name of a good guitar teacher. When you did, he strongly suggested you learn to play the flute instead. You have no interest in the flute. Your parents are fine with your learning the guitar. But the teacher insists the flute is a better instrument. What's more, he expects you to follow his advice because, as he says, "I'm an adult, and I know more than you do."

Why is this a dilemma?

You've been taught not to disobey adults. You've been taught not to hurt someone's feelings. By not taking his advice, at the very least you might hurt this man's feelings. It also might be considered disobedience. But yet you *know* that what he's told you to do is not the best advice for you.

If you think of a solution, but it isn't a good one, what is the problem with that solution?

You could tell him, "Thanks. I'll remember what you

said," then do what you know is best anyhow.

There are two problems here. One is that maybe, while his suggestion isn't a good one for you, your plan isn't the best one either. Some other instrument altogether might be better for you. The other is that he might follow up and ask you, in a week or so, if you've started your flute lessons yet. *Then* what do you tell him?

Is there a way around the problem?

If this is not a situation where he expects you to follow his advice right then, you can always say, "Thank you for the advice," then discuss the situation with one of your parents (or another trusted adult who is knowledgeable on the subject). By getting another opinion from an adult, you accomplish two things. One: You might get a different opinion altogether – and one that feels right to you. Two: If the music teacher asks you later whether you've started your flute lessons yet, you'll have a better answer for him. You can say, "My parents really want me to learn guitar," or "My sister's piano teacher thinks I'd be good at the cello, and I'm going to try that."

DILEMMA 3

A grownup neighbor is cruel to his dog. You want to talk to him about it. Your friend says you had better mind your own business.

Why is this a dilemma?

You haven't got the right to tell a grownup how to behave. Yet if you don't speak up to help that poor dog, who's going to?

If you think of a solution, but it isn't a good one, what is the problem with that solution?

You could leave a note for the neighbor and not sign it. Tell him you know he's cruel to the dog. Tell him you're watching him.

But if he's cruel, and he finds out you're the one who

wrote the note, he might do something to you, too. Or maybe, if he realizes it's a kid's handwriting, he might just ignore the note.

Is there a way around the problem?

You need to tell a grownup – one of your parents – who can report this cruel neighbor to the SPCA (Society for the Prevention of Cruelty to Animals) or whatever local city or government agency would be the best to step in and do something to help protect the dog.

DILEMMA 4

Your friend's mom has invited you to stay for dinner. But you discover – too late – that she's serving your least favorite food. Or, even more serious, there may be reasons why you simply *can't* eat what your friend's mom offers you.

Suppose you're allergic to tomatoes, which are in the salad? Suppose you're lactose-intolerant, and the cauliflower was cooked in a cheese sauce? Suppose you're from a kosher Jewish or observant Moslem home and can't eat the roast pork for religious reasons?

Why is this a dilemma?

Let's take this one situation at a time. If it's simply a matter of your not liking the food, what are you going to do? Your mom has taught you not to say you hate foods. But you really don't like to eat fish, or liver, or lamb – whatever it is your friend's mom has prepared. And if you really *can't* eat the food, for health or religious reasons? You still know your mom wouldn't want you to make a problem for your hostess – even though Mom wouldn't want you eating the food, either.

If you think of a solution, but it isn't a good one, what is the problem with that solution?

You could try to force yourself to eat the lamb (or whatever the food is) anyhow. But if you have trouble getting it down, your friend's mom is going to realize it. Then she might think it's *her cooking* you don't like, rather than *that particular food.*

You could eat the pork and hope God would understand you were trying to be mannerly and not make problems. Certainly God wants us to have good manners and not make problems. But you wouldn't feel right about it.

You could eat the cheese or tomatoes and hope you didn't have too bad an allergic reaction. But should you really have to suffer in an attempt to have good manners?

Is there a way around the problem?

Yes – this is a case where honesty really is the best policy. Again, let's talk about simple dislikes first. You can say something like, "I'm sorry. I don't usually eat lamb. I don't really like it. But maybe you make it better than my mom does. May I try a very small piece?"

At best, you'll find that your friend's mom *does* cook lamb in a way you like better. After you've tasted it, you'll ask for a little more. Your friend's mom will feel flattered. If you don't like it, well, you've warned her you don't care for that particular food, so she shouldn't feel insulted if you don't have any more of it. As long as you don't make a face and say, "Oh, gross... lamb! Yuuck!" you're not guilty of bad manners.

But what if it's a matter of an allergy or a religious belief? Well, then, your friend's mom certainly will understand. If you say, "I'm sorry, but I'm not allowed to eat tomatoes. I'm allergic," or "I'm sorry, but I'm not allowed to eat pork. We're kosher," you're not creating the situation yourself. You're not being fussy, or difficult, or stubborn.

The key things to remember here are:

- Apologize for not eating the food that's a problem for you.
- Explain your reason briefly.
- Don't ask your friend's mom to cook something else for you. Eat whatever else she serves that you can eat, and have a nibble of something more when you get home if you're still hungry. There's probably yogurt in your fridge or cereal in your cabinet that will fill up the empty space in your stomach.

And as long as you make do with whatever else your friend's mom serves – vegetables and potatoes, or soup and salad – you're not being a difficult guest.

PART 4

Everyday Dilemmas

DILEMMA 1

Your teacher asks you to stay after school and talk to her about the trouble you're having in your History class. But she is called away over the P.A. system just as she sits down. She tells you she'll be right back. You are standing right in front of her desk and you can see the test for tomorrow is lying right there. If you peek, you'll know what the questions and answers are!

Why is this a dilemma?

If you know what the questions and answers are, you can get a better grade – and you need all the help you can get! But you know you're not supposed to peek at the test.

If you think of a solution, but it isn't a good one, what is the problem with that solution?

If you only look at what the questions are and don't copy the answers, somehow it doesn't seem as bad. You could get the answers to the questions out of your History book later on, and then you'd actually be learning something, so isn't that a *good* thing?

But you know you aren't supposed to peek. It's still a form of cheating. And none of the other kids knows what the questions are, so you have an unfair advantage.

Is there a way around the problem?

Honesty is the only answer. As tempting as it is to peek, you mustn't. If you do badly on the test, at least you'll know you were honest. If you do well, you'll have gotten the good mark fairly.

And if you cheat and peek, then get a good mark this once, and do badly again on the next test, the teacher might suspect something. She isn't stupid. And the teacher knows you were alone in the room while the test was sitting there on the desk.

DILEMMA 2

Your parents ask you to do a load of laundry as soon as you finish your homework. You say you will, and you go upstairs to do your homework. But you need to call one of your friends to ask a question about an assignment, and in the process, you start talking about something else entirely. Pretty soon forty-five minutes have gone by.

You're upstairs, and your parents are downstairs. They don't realize you've been on the phone at all. You finally start to do your homework. But then you get distracted checking your e-mail. You find a message that has to be answered right away. After a while, you realize it's getting really late.

You log off and get back to your homework. But by now it's almost your bedtime. Your mom sticks her head in the door and says, "Still doing your homework, honey? I didn't know you had that much. All right, I'll do the laundry for you."

Why is this a dilemma?

Because you got out of doing a chore, and now your mom's doing it for you – but it all happened through a bit of dishonesty. Your mom thinks you were doing homework all that time, and you weren't. You didn't tell any lies, but you also didn't speak up and tell the truth.

If you think of a solution, but it isn't a good one, what is the problem with that solution?

You could go downstairs and tell your mom, "I wasn't doing my homework the whole time. I got distracted by a phone call and checking my e-mail. I'll do the laundry right now."

She might be angry with you for not getting everything done in time and goofing off before your work was finished. And since she wants you to go to bed on time, she probably won't let you do the laundry anyhow.

Is there a way around the problem?

You can go downstairs and tell her honestly, "Listen, I had to call a friend to ask something about the homework, and we got to talking, and that's part of why my homework isn't done yet. I know that was wrong. I also know it's too late for me to do the laundry tonight, but I owe you one. I'll do the laundry the next time you want it done, OK? I'm sorry."

Your mom will respect your honesty and probably not get on your case big-time about goofing off. And you'll have a clear conscience.

DILEMMA 3

There's a girl in your class who uses a wheelchair. Mom says to always be sensitive and considerate of people who have problems like that. Trouble is, you really don't like Sandra. It has nothing to do with her wheelchair – she just isn't a very nice person, and she isn't a very interesting person, and you don't have anything in common. Sandra asks you over to her house after school one day.

Why is this a dilemma?

If you say "No," she might think it's because of her disability. But the truth is, you really just don't want to be Sandra's friend.

If you think of a solution, but it isn't a good one, what is the problem with that solution?

Go over to her house this once. Bring a friend. Spend more time with the friend than with Sandra. Leave early.

But, in the first place, Sandra might expect you to invite her to your house next time. In the second place, if you and your friend spend more time with each other than with Sandra, she's going to feel more left out than ever.

Is there a way around the problem?

There's a difference between being considerate and sensitive to someone and pitying them. Sandra doesn't want your pity. She wants your friendship. And apparently she isn't a great person. If you went to her house, it would be out of pity, not out of really liking her. You'll have to gently tell her "No," you don't want to come over to her place after school.

So be nice to her in school. Maybe even invite her to your next birthday party. But you don't have to be friends with her. Friendship shouldn't be based on pity.

Just be sure you're considerate of her in school and never do anything that could leave her thinking you're avoiding her because of her wheelchair.

DILEMMA 4

It's Christmas time, and your class is having a gift exchange. Everyone draws someone else's name out of a bag. Nobody knows who got whose name. You got Tara.

Nobody likes Tara. You yourself don't really dislike Tara, but you're certainly not her friend. You think about giving her something nasty. Wouldn't it be hilarious if Tara opens her gift and finds... plastic doggy poop? Or something equally funny?

Even if nobody knows it was you, everyone will laugh. And if you tell some of the other kids that it was you who gave Tara the plastic poop, you know you'll be more popular than ever.

Why is this a dilemma?

You know that the rest of the kids will cheer you on for giving Tara a nasty present in the Christmas gift exchange. But you also know that it's not nice to give a nasty gift. You want the other kids' approval. But do you really want to do something nasty? Especially at Christmas time – though for that matter, at any time.

If you think of a solution, but it isn't a good one, what is the problem with that solution?

You can give Tara a serious present, a nice present, but your friend Pam knows that you drew Tara's name in the gift exchange, and Pam keeps urging you to give Tara something nasty. "Won't it be so perfect when she opens the gift!" Pam keeps saying. You want Pam's approval.

Is there a way around the problem?

Suppose you were Tara? Would *you* like getting plastic dog poop or some other dumb, nasty gift? You don't have to spend big money to get Tara the nicest present in the store, but give the girl a break! It's Christmas! Besides, what has Tara ever done to you? She may not be the best-liked girl in school, but has she ever done anything mean to you? No? Then why do something mean to her?

If Pam says anything to you, you should remind her that it's Christmas. Where's Pam's Christmas spirit? What has Tara ever done to Pam?

CONCLUSION

Getting a Handle on Other Dilemmas

Now that you've read this book, you have ideas about how to handle some of the difficult situations you might face in your life. But even more than that, you've learned how to think them through. This will help you with *other* difficult situations. If you find yourself in a dilemma that I haven't described here, you'll be able to think your way through it by asking yourself:

- What is the problem?
- What are some possible solutions?
- What might be wrong with those solutions?
- What might be a better solution?

Use your brain. Think creatively and you can think your way through many dilemmas in life.

And nobody gets the answer right to *every* dilemma.

Finally, here's one last – and much bigger – dilemma. Read on carefully.

You become aware of a problem that you really feel needs to have something done about it – and yet really don't know what to do. If you do the wrong thing, you and/or someone else could wind up with a bigger problem on your or their hands. Do you try to speak out or do something anyhow? If so, what? Or should you just try to forget the whole thing? Now you're *really* in a dilemma and you *really* don't feel comfortable simply ignoring the situation.

On the other hand, maybe your gut instinct is telling you that you just can't find a way to fix the problem yourself. If you try, you might make things worse for someone... or you might get yourself into a really difficult or even dangerous situation.

Look at the different dilemma scenarios below. In each of these cases, you feel someone needs your help, or a bad situation needs reporting, or you have important information that needs to be given to someone who's in a better position to act than you.

What to do?

First of all, what sorts of situations am I talking about? I'll give you a few examples, though that's all they are – examples. There are certainly plenty of other such situations that would fall into the same category.

Situation 1

The kid next door is older than you, so you're not particularly friends. One day, when you're in your back yard, you see him sneak onto the screened-in back patio of the neighbors on the other side. He doesn't realize you're watching, but you see him steal a laptop computer or video game box from that neighbor's house.

Since you have no real friendship with this kid and he's older than you, you don't think it would do much good to go up to him and say, "I saw what you did. Now put it back." Besides, if he's the sort who would steal, he might also be the sort who would do something nasty to you. On the other hand, if you just ignore the whole thing, someone's going to be without their computer – and all the valuable files and data on it. Replacing the computer would be expensive. Replacing everything on the hard drive would be totally impossible. Or maybe the video game box is something you know the kid next door saved up all his paper route money to buy, and it means almost everything to him.

Situation 2

Your best friend, Barry, tells you that his football coach has been inviting some of the team members over to his house. At first you think it's great that the coach is cool. But after a while, some of the things Barry tells you doesn't sound right. Maybe Coach is inviting the guys over one by one, not as a group. Or maybe he's been asking them some rather personal questions. Or maybe Barry says that Coach has a habit of touching him often – a bit more than you feel is appropriate.

Whatever the exact information is you're getting, you're not comfortable with it. And yet Coach hasn't done anything that very clearly crosses the line between friendly and just plain wrong. What to do? Suppose he is just being friendly. If you report him, you'll probably get him in BIG trouble... maybe for no reason. (Who would you report him to anyhow? And what would you report? He hasn't done anything clearly wrong.) Yet you know something about this situation feels all wrong, even though Barry might not agree with you. And you don't want Barry – or any of the other guys – to have to deal with it by themselves if Coach does have intentions that aren't appropriate.

Scenario 3

You're biking with a friend. A car comes along and grazes your friend's bike tire, knocking him to the ground. Fortunately, your friend is only bruised and scraped. He's eventually able to get up and ride home. But the driver of the car never stops to make sure he's all right.

You make a mental note of the make of car, the color, and even the first few numbers of the license plate. But now what do you do?

Scenario 4

A kid in school keeps saying she wishes she were dead. She says she doesn't care if she lives or not; she doesn't enjoy life anyhow. You're afraid she might be thinking of killing herself, but you don't know this for a fact. You don't know her parents, either. You feel you ought to do something, but you haven't a clue what to do.

Scenario 5

You notice one of your friends sometimes has black-and-blue marks, or other injuries. She's no longer willing to change clothes in front of you for gym class, or when she comes to your house for a sleep-over. You wonder if she's hiding more injuries. She says she just falls down a lot, runs into furniture, doesn't watch where she's going. But you wonder if someone is doing this to her. You'd like to protect her – if she needs protection. But you can't be sure, and anyhow she doesn't seem to want help. Yet, if the situation is what you're afraid it is, how can you let it go on without doing something? *What do you do?*

In each of these situations, you have to do something. Why?

• Because it's the right thing to do, morally.

• Because you have information that could help someone else.

• Because if it were *your* laptop computer (or your parents'), or your video game box, wouldn't you want to get it back? Because if Coach really is some sort of molester, do you want your best friend – or any other kid – to be his victim? Because if you were the person whom the hit-and-run driver injured, even though you weren't hurt badly, wouldn't you want the police to catch the guilty person? Don't you want them to make him or her go to court for what they did? And maybe take away their driver's license or make them pay a fine? Because if the girl who you think is suicidal does kill herself, her life is over – and her family is going to be going through unbelievable grief over it, too; and there's no way to make things better after *that* happens. Because if the girl with the bruises really is being physically abused by a parent, she needs help! – even if she's afraid to ask for it.

OK, it certainly looks like there are some serious reasons for not just turning your back and trying to forget you saw anything. But what should you do?

You need to do the same thing an adult does when he (or she) is in over his (or her) head – you need to *get help.*

Getting help can be as simple as telling a parent or some other adult.

Who are the adults you can go to for help with serious situations?

• Your parents

• Another close relative (an aunt or uncle, for example, or an adult brother or sister)

• A teacher, principal, or guidance counselor at school

• A clergyperson (pastor or minister, rabbi or cantor, or priest)

• A police officer

If, for whatever reason, you feel you can't easily turn to any of these adults, you should find a well-known, respected organization that specializes in helping kids or in dealing with the sort of situation you're facing. Below you will find a few really useful phone numbers and Web sites of organizations that exist to help kids faced with these kinds of really tough dilemmas. Keep these phone numbers, e-mail addresses, and Web sites handy.

Help! (and where to find it) – Helpful Hotlines and Web Sites

- ***Befrienders International***

www.befrienders.org

This is a place you can go to online to get help with really heavy issues including: suicide, depression, self-harm, homosexuality, and bullying. Befrienders is based in London, England, but has 371 support centers throughout the world, in forty-one countries. The Web site information is available in fourteen different languages. It has an excellent directory of suicide and crisis help lines.

- ***www.Freevibe.com***

This U.S.-based anti-drug Web site is a joint venture between Disney and the Office for National Drug Control Policy (U.S. Government Public Health Service). The site is cool and unpatronizing. It promotes a drug-free lifestyle for kids (preteens and teens). Here you can find tons of up-to-date articles, discussions, games, polls, and celebrity news. See what other teens are saying about drugs and violence, and about the benefits of a drug-free lifestyle.

- ***Girls and Boys Town***

http://www.girlsandboystown.org/home.asp

This respected organization has two 24 hour hotlines for many different problems and offers crisis counseling. You can call them at 1-800-448-3000, or 1-800-448-1833. Girls and Boys Town has been around for over eighty-five years and is a U.S. leader in the care and treatment of abused, abandoned, and neglected kids. Among the many help services they offer, they're specialists in helping kids who are thinking of suicide. The 24 hour hotlines are staffed by trained counselors every day of the year. The Web site has a really useful chatroom, tips, and useful links.

- ***Kids Help Online***

www.kidshelp.org

This U.S.-based Web site has a great database, a wealth of info, and an enormous list of hotlines. Chat rooms are monitored by professionals, and all resources and links are routinely checked.

- ***Kids Help Phone (Canada) Hotline: 1-800-668-6868***

http://www.kidshelp.sympatico.ca/

***Available in French too.**

This Canadian hotline has counselors available twenty-four hours a day, every single day of the year. All the counselors have access to a database of thirty thousand Canadian community and social service organizations from coast to coast.

They also have a program for adult support – for parents and caregivers – called Parent Help Line.

- ***The National Child Abuse Hotline: 1-800-422-4453***

Counselors take calls twenty-four hours a day, seven days a week from anywhere in the U.S. or Canada.

I hope you never need this information. But if you ever need it, now you have it. And if you do ever need it... ***use it!***

Good luck!

Look for these other titles in Lobster Press' "Millennium Generation Series" at your local bookseller:

When I Grow Up,
I Want to Be a Writer
by Cynthia MacGregor
ISBN: 1-894222-42-3

7 Secrets of Highly
Successful Kids
by Peter Kuitenbrouwer
ISBN: 1-894222-39-3

The S(ex) Book:
An Alphabet of Smarter Love
by Jane Pavanel
ISBN: 1-894222-30-X

Make Things Happen:
The Key to Networking for
Teens
by Lara Zielin
ISBN: 1-894222-43-1